# ABOUT THE AUTHOR

Jessica Bell is an award-winning author/poet, writing/publishing coach, graphic designer, and singer-songwriter who was born in Melbourne, Australia. She currently resides in Athens, Greece.

In addition to having published a memoir, four novels, three poetry collections, and her bestselling Writing in a Nutshell series, she has been featured in a variety of publications and ABC Radio National shows such as *Writer's Digest*, *Publisher's Weekly*, *The Guardian*, *Life Matters*, and *Poetica*.

She is also the Publisher of Vine Leaves Press, CEO of Independent Publishing Assistance, a voice-over actor, and the coordinator of the Writing Day Workshops.

In October 2016, she became the new lead singer of the well-known dream-pop group, Keep Shelly In Athens, and records and performs as a solo artist under the name BRUNO.

Visit: *iamjessicabell.com*

# ADVERBS & CLICHÉS
## IN A
## NUTSHELL

### DEMONSTRATED SUBVERSION OF
### ADVERBS & CLICHÉS INTO GOURMET IMAGERY

## Jessica Bell

**Vine Leaves Press**
Melbourne, Vic, Australia

**ADVERBS & CLICHÉS IN A NUTSHELL:**
**Demonstrated Subversion of Adverbs & Clichés into Gourmet Imagery**

Copyright © 2019 Second Edition Jessica Bell
All rights reserved.
ISBN: 978-1-925965-03-2

First published 2013 Jessica Bell

Published by Vine Leaves Press, 2019
Melbourne, Vic, Australia

All prose examples are fiction. Any similarity between the characters and situations within its pages and places or persons, living or dead, is unintentional and co-incidental.

Cover and interior design by Jessica Bell

A catalogue record for this book is available from the National Library of Australia

# CONTENTS

# INTRODUCTION

Writers constantly have rules thrown at them left, right, and center. Show, don't tell! Stop using so many dialogue tags! More sensory detail! More tension! Speed up the pace! Yada yada yada it can become overwhelming, yes? I used to feel overwhelmed by it all too. In fact, I still do sometimes. It's hard enough to get the words on the page, let alone consider how to put them there.

My own struggles have led me to write this series of pocket-sized writing guides. So you can learn to hone your craft in bite-sized, manageable pieces. But please keep in mind, their purpose is to inspire you to become better at your craft. To teach you how to grow as a writer. They will not tell you how to write. They will not preach writing rules and styles to you. But they will help you realize that you can, little by little, end up with a work of fiction as unique as your own soul (whether you regard your soul as a spiritual entity, or nobility of temperament, in this context it is one and the same).

I like to think of a writer's "voice" as the soul of their imagi-nation. If you stay true to your soul, you will produce unique fiction. There is no doubt about it. Because everyone has his or her own soul. No other soul in this world will ever possess the exact same qualities as yours. So when you are seeking writing advice, always take into account that the advice is coming from writers with their own unique souls, too. Be inspired by them. Feel motivated. But do not feel the need to be like them. Trying to write like somebody else is (bar writing exercises), in my opinion, the biggest disservice you can do for your work.

In the first part of this book, I focussed on demonstrating how to transition "telling" into "showing." In this part, I deal with another of the most common criticisms aspiring writers face: to absolutely avoid adverbs and clichés like the plague. But see, right now, I just used one of each. And at the beginning of the Introduction, I used a few too. Because they come naturally, and we frequently use them in everyday speech. But in fiction, too many adverbs and clichés weaken your prose. It's considered "lazy writing," because it means we don't have to show what's happening.

If your manuscript has too many adverbs and clichés, it most likely means that the emotion you felt while writing it is not going to translate to the reader in the same way. Never underestimate the weakness of adverbs and clichés. You'd be surprised how vivid your writing will become once they are subverted.

Sure, clichés exist because they stem from things many of us experience in real life, and you may argue that they are "relatable," so why not use them? But the way in which one experiences things isn't always the same. As writers, it's your duty to make readers experience your story from a unique point of view. Your point of view.

Before we go into details about how adverbs and clichés weaken prose, and how you can subvert them, first you need to understand that they aren't always going to be a problem. In fact, you don't need to go overboard trying to eliminate every single adverb and cliché in your manuscript. Because sometimes, they just work. They serve a purpose. Especially in dialogue. Of course, it also depends a lot on your character's voice.

For example, sometimes it's more concise to write, "She knocked lightly on the door." Not every single action needs to be poetic and unique. Sometimes you need to write exactly what someone is doing because it's not important enough to draw attention to. Also, if we just wrote, "She knocked on the door," we'd have no idea whether it was loud or not. And if this action wasn't all that significant, it would be a bit too wordy to say something like, "She knocked on the door as if her hand were as light as a feather." (Look, cliché again, they creep in so easily, don't they?)

But consider this: What if this person's light knocking on the door was paramount to the story? What if it was a moment of suspense? What if behind that door was a man this person was afraid of? What if this person was anticipating being verbally abused for the interruption? Then this "lightly knocking on the door" would have a significant purpose, yes?

The action of lightly knocking on that door is no longer a simple transitional action that moves the character from A to B. It is in your manuscript for a reason. You put it there for your readers to feel the same apprehension your character feels. And no adverb or cliché, as you can see, is going to draw attention to that moment of intensity like something crafted for it exclusively.

So let's try our hand at making this moment pop. How about, "She tapped on the door. It echoed in her ears like an axe to a carcass."

So how does this better convey its intended sentiment? I'd say the fact that this person perceives their tap on the door as a deep, echoing, and unpleasant sound means that they are anxious about the reaction it is going to elicit. Also note that I've chosen the verb (tap) which means "a light knock," so there is no reason for me to use the adverb "lightly."

So how exactly can we approach the subversion of adverbs and clichés? For starters, play around with similes and metaphors when you're trying to convey emotion, and for action, use strong verbs to show it happening in real time. For example, instead of using something clichéd like "the streets were so quiet you could hear a pin drop," find a small detail to zoom in on that shows how quiet the streets are. Put a lonely-looking man kicking rubbish down an abandoned street, perhaps. Have him drag his feet. Perhaps the sound can be heard from two blocks away where your narrator is waiting for a bus that never arrives.

Most of the time, if you think of the small details, rather than the bigger picture, you'll avoid adverbs and clichés naturally. And remember to be experimental. You never know what you might come up with.

By analyzing the thirty-four subversions of adverbs and clichés in this part, I hope you will be inspired to transform the mundane and overused expressions in your work into gourmet imagery.

I suggest you follow these steps:

**Step one:** For the first read-through, read each example in its entirety, to grasp the general feel of them. Notice how flat the examples using the adverbs and clichés sound compared to the unique examples.

**Step two:** For the second read-through, identify which elements in the unique examples match the basic sentiments of the adverbs and clichés presented in the other examples.

**Step three:** For the third read-through, identify how the unique example conveys, and/or adds to, those sentiments.

**Step four:** And for the fourth and final read-through, brainstorm your own way of subverting the examples that use the adverbs and clichés. Remember, do not try to write like me. Just be yourself. Close the book. Close your eyes. Immerse yourself in the situation.

In this print edition, I have provided some blank lined pages at the back of the book for you to jot down your notes and ideas as you read.

Three short writing prompts are also provided.

There are also separate alphabetical indexes of adverbs, and clichés.

Happy subverting!

# EXAMPLE 1

**Adverbs:** loudly • relentlessly • slowly

**Clichés:** scream like a hyena • snail's pace
• splitting headache • traffic jam

## USING ADVERBS

I slowly move through the chaotic traffic, my daughter screaming loudly in the back seat. My head is throbbing relentlessly. It feels like it's going to crack open.

## USING CLICHÉS

My daughter and I are stuck in a traffic jam, and it's giving me a splitting headache. The cars are moving at a snail's pace, and my daughter is screaming like a hyena.

## UNIQUE EXAMPLE

The sharp shrill of car horns and my daughter's wails pierce through my head like ice picks, doing nothing to help lessen my grip on the steering wheel, while we inch along in grueling traffic.

# EXAMPLE 2

**Adverb:** habitually

**Cliché:** old habits die hard

## USING ADVERB

Men are habitually stubborn.

## USING CLICHÉ

Men never change. Old habits die hard.

## UNIQUE EXAMPLE

Men cling to habit like sap to a tree trunk.

# EXAMPLE 3

**Adverb:** badly

**Cliché:** leave a bad taste in one's mouth

## USING ADVERB

His behaviour affected me badly.

## USING CLICHÉ

His behaviour left me with a bad taste in my mouth.

## UNIQUE EXAMPLE

The aftermath of his behaviour plagued my senses like rotten egg.

# EXAMPLE 4

**Adverbs:** desperately • finally • freely • heavily • lightly

**Clichés:** as light as a feather • clean slate • feel the weight on one's shoulders • under the skin

## USING ADVERBS

As I lightly step onto the sand, I realize I'm finally ready to start over, far from the place where I desperately feel the need to run away. I'll head to a town where regret no longer weighs heavily on me; a place where I can freely be myself.

## USING CLICHÉS

I step foot onto the sand, my feet as light as feathers. I realize I'm ready for a clean slate, to start again in a new town where I no longer feel the weight of regret on my shoulders, or the strong desire to flee; a place where I'll be accepted for who I am under the skin.

## UNIQUE EXAMPLE

As I tiptoe out of the water, I am weightless. I'm ready to wipe this regret from my skin; to immerse myself in a new ocean, where my desire for fleeing this emotional cage hides like a mermaid ambivalent about growing legs. I'll never have to disguise my soul again.

# EXAMPLE 5

**Adverb:** sluggishly

**Cliché:** dead weight

## USING ADVERB

Her clammy hands rest sluggishly in mine.

## USING CLICHÉ

Her sweaty hands rest in mine like dead weight.

## UNIQUE EXAMPLE

Her hands rest in mine like damp autumn leaves.

# EXAMPLE 6

**Adverbs:** angrily • suddenly

**Clichés:** bristle with rage • make one's hair stand on end

## USING ADVERBS

"How dare you," Frank says angrily. Suddenly, I feel scared.

## USING CLICHÉS

Frank is bristling with so much rage that it makes my hair stand on end.

## UNIQUE EXAMPLE

"How dare you." Frank growls and swipes everything off my desk. The air thickens in my throat like starch in water.

# EXAMPLE 7

**Adverbs:** always • intensely • nervously • thoroughly • truly

**Clichés:** break out in a cold sweat • bundle of nerves • deep down • get a kick out of • give it one's all • if you do it once, you'll do it again

## USING ADVERBS

Stage fright is an intensely rooted fear. But despite being anxious all the time, I truly know that I thoroughly enjoy performing in front of a live audience. Once I've done it, I'll be addicted and always need another hit. And I'll no longer linger nervously at the side of the stage.

## USING CLICHÉS

Despite stage fright making me break out in a cold sweat, deep down I know I get a kick out of singing for a live audience. It's like a drug: if I do it once, I want to do it again. I'm no longer a bundle of nerves, and the need to give it my all is paramount.

## UNIQUE EXAMPLE

Stage fright is a paralytic, a dude stiffened by tetrodotoxin. But the overall thrill of singing for a live audience survives the poison, and I wake up on the other side, ready to get back on stage. With the angst gone, the craving to perform again overpowers me like a vampire needs blood.

# EXAMPLE 8

**Adverb:** attentively • closely • constantly

**Clichés:** alarms go off in one's head • gut instinct
• ignore the signs

## USING ADVERB

No matter how many warnings I get, I constantly ignore them. Maybe I should  closely and attentively listen to my instincts.

## USING CLICHÉS

I should stop ignoring the signs. Alarms keep going off in my head, but I just don't listen to my gut instincts.

## UNIQUE EXAMPLE

I should listen to the elusive buzz of caution, instead of flicking it away like a fly interrupting my concentration.

# EXAMPLE 9

**Adverb:** faintly

**Cliché:** hear in the distance

## USING ADVERB

The clock ticks faintly in the background.

## USING CLICHÉ

I can hear the clock ticking in the distance.

## UNIQUE EXAMPLE

The clock ticks like a sewing needle tapping eggshell.

# EXAMPLE 10

**Adverbs:** emotionally • morbidly • perpetually • strikingly • stylishly • woefully

**Clichés:** down in the mouth • dressed to kill • keep at bay • ooh and ahh • put pressure on oneself • sense of self-pride

## USING ADVERBS

I stare at myself, dressed stylishly in black, in the TV screen. There's something morbidly beautiful and dark about my reflection and how it woefully matches the ambivalence I feel about myself right now. Wouldn't it be great if I could perpetually stay in there? I'd be praised by others all day long for my strikingly stunning pose, and abolish my judgmental inner-voice. I might feel emotionally stable again.

## USING CLICHÉS

I stare at my reflection in the TV screen. Though I may be dressed to kill, I sure don't feel that way. I feel down in the mouth and insecure about myself, but I feel a small sense of self-pride too. I wish I was a painting on a wall. Onlookers would ooh and ahh at my striking gothic beauty, and I'd stop putting so much pressure on myself to please others. I might keep my emotional instability at bay.

## UNIQUE EXAMPLE

The TV is off. I stare at my reflection in the screen. I'm an eighteenth-century portrait on canvas, in a grey hue, as if painted in darkness. Much like the darkness I live inside my head. If only I could remain in that reflection—motionless, flushed with gothic candor, a drifter in a place where I will never judge myself; a place where I can be hung in a gallery and praised rather than scrutinized for my unconventional individuality.

# EXAMPLE 11

**Adverbs:** practically • remarkably • smoothly • sweetly

**Clichés:** eye candy • so (adj) one could eat it

## USING ADVERBS

Mike is remarkably handsome, and he speaks so smoothly and sweetly in his British accent, I can practically taste it.

## USING CLICHÉS

Mike is pure eye candy, and his British accent is so smooth and sweet I could just eat it.

## UNIQUE EXAMPLE

Mike's picture should be on the front page of Who. And you should hear him speak. His British accent is like crème caramel.

# EXAMPLE 12

**Adverb:** rhythmically

**Cliché:** to the beat of one's heart

## USING ADVERB

Eli rhythmically flicks a teaspoon in his palm.

## USING CLICHÉ

Eli flicks a teaspoon in his palm to the beat of my heart.

## UNIQUE EXAMPLE

Eli flicks a teaspoon in his palm. It thumps like a weak heart in a distant stethoscope.

# EXAMPLE 13

**Adverbs:** coolly • creatively • extremely • genuinely • positively • utterly

**Clichés:** elixir of life • flight of fancy • have a gift • in one's blood • it's not a crime • one can dream • pause in thought • unvarnished truth • vivid imagination

## USING ADVERBS

"My presence is so positively calming, your daughter wishes she could drink it." Dr. Morris smiled coolly. "Of course, that is an utterly unrealistic yearning, but she likes to creatively express herself. And I do not believe this to be a threat to her psychological well-being. I believe observations such as these are extremely intelligent." Dr. Morris seemed genuinely pleased with my daughter's progress, but I wasn't convinced.

## USING CLICHÉS

"My presence makes your daughter feel so calm, she claims it could be her elixir of life." Dr. Morris had no qualms about telling us the unvarnished truth of our daughter's psychological health. "Of course, this is merely a flight of fancy, but one can dream, yes? Regardless, having such a vivid imagination is in her blood. It's not a crime." Dr. Morris pauses in thought. "In fact, I believe she may have a gift."

## UNIQUE EXAMPLE

"My companionship seems to instill a sense of calm in your daughter. I quote: 'I wish I could catch your presence in a jar, leave it on my mantle, and take self-prescribed sips from it when needed.' Extraordinary, yes?" Dr. Morris nodded, as if trying to convince himself that her remark was worthy of admiration. "It may seem idealistic, but everybody's minds do indeed adjust one's reality to fulfill one's emotional needs." He smiles, squints at a painting on his wall. "I don't believe there is anything wrong with being so imaginative. No. No, not at all."

# EXAMPLE 14

**Adverbs:** furiously • totally

**Clichés:** behave like (n) is invisible • blow a gasket

## USING ADVERBS

My colleagues totally ignore me. It makes me furiously mad.

## USING CLICHÉS

My colleagues get on with their work as if I'm invisible. I think I'm going to blow a gasket.

## UNIQUE EXAMPLE

My colleagues' persistent disregard for my presence pisses me off like an un-locatable itch.

# EXAMPLE 15

**Adverb:** tremendously

**Cliché:** I could eat a horse

## USING ADVERB

I'm tremendously hungry.

## USING CLICHÉ

I'm so hungry I could eat a horse.

## UNIQUE EXAMPLE

If you put me in an eating contest, I'd win. Not only would I win, I'd go out for dinner afterward to celebrate!

# EXAMPLE 16

**Adverbs:** eventually • merrily • recklessly

**Clichés:** as happy as Larry (AmE: a clam) • as tough as nails
• before you know it • black and blue • do (n) like there's no
tomorrow • go hell for leather

## USING ADVERBS

My three-year-old son is sitting merrily on my shoulders at
the party. He thinks I'm as strong as daddy and recklessly
swings his arms and legs around to the music, kicking and
punching me everywhere, oblivious to the damage he's doing.
Eventually, my chest is covered in ghastly bruises.

## USING CLICHÉS

My three-year-old son is as happy as Larry sitting on my
shoulders at the party. He thinks I'm as tough as nails, just
like daddy, and goes hell for leather, swinging his arms and
legs around to the music like there's no tomorrow. Before I
know it, my chest is black and blue.

## UNIQUE EXAMPLE

My three-year-old son and I are at the party. I feel vibrations in
my shoulders as he giggles to the music. But sometimes I think
he forgets who he's sitting on and swings his limbs around like
a rag doll in a washing machine. Before long, bruises stain my
chest like a white blouse washed with black socks.

# EXAMPLE 17

**Adverb:** mournfully

**Cliché:** bawl one's eyes out

## USING ADVERB

I'm weeping mournfully.

## USING CLICHÉ

I'm so sad that I bawl my eyes out.

## UNIQUE EXAMPLE

My tears erupt like storm water from a cracked drain pipe.

# EXAMPLE 18

**Adverb:** tragically

**Cliché:** pour one's heart out

## USING ADVERB

The clarinet sounds tragically sad in this song.

## USING CLICHÉ

The clarinet in this song sounds like it's pouring its heart out.

## UNIQUE EXAMPLE

In this song, the clarinet is a wilting willow, pleading to be left in solitude to wither and fade.

# EXAMPLE 19

**Adverbs:** frankly • persistently • somewhat • successfully

**Clichés:** achieve one's goals • clutching at
(AmE: grasping for) straws • no pain, no gain • reach for the
stars • run into obstacles • see the light at the end of the tunnel
• so be it

## USING ADVERBS

I've persistently been doing everything and anything I can
to reach my goals successfully. Yeah, my goals are somewhat
impossible to achieve, but so what? I like the challenge.
Frankly, I only have one wish. If I can't get what I want
without a struggle, then please give me an obstacle that I can
at least overcome. I can't cope with moving backward all the
time.

## USING CLICHÉS

All these years, I've been clutching at straws to achieve my
goals. Sure, I've been reaching for the stars, and they're a long
way away. But no pain, no gain, right? If I can't get what I
want without running into anymore obstacles, then so be it.
But give me one that I can overcome, so that I can at least see
the light at the end of the tunnel.

## UNIQUE EXAMPLE

All these years, I've been trying to cross an ocean via a never-ending bridge made of fraying string. My goals may seem unrealistic to some. Though I walk backward sometimes, I haven't slipped off the bridge. Yet. All I long for is the day when my only obstacle is a narrow creek I can drop a plank of wood over. I can even fall in if you like. I don't care if I get all muddy. As long as I make it across.

# EXAMPLE 20

**Adverbs:** completely • sleepily

**Clichés:** close, but no cigar • dog-tired

## USING ADVERBS

I sleepily reach for my mobile phone, but my coordination is completely off and I grab my hair brush instead.

## USING CLICHÉS

Still dog-tired, I reach for my mobile phone on the bedside table. Close, but no cigar.

## UNIQUE EXAMPLE

I reach for the mobile phone on my bedside table as if my hand were a sea lion flipper.

# EXAMPLE 21

**Adverb:** rapidly

**Cliché:** racing heart

## USING ADVERB

My heart beats rapidly.

## USING CLICHÉ

My heart races.

## UNIQUE EXAMPLE

My heart beats like a cog train gaining speed.

# EXAMPLE 22

**Adverbs:** barely • definitely • hardly • painfully • really • very • violently

**Clichés:** in way over one's head • off the charts • speck of dust • the best of one's ability • time flies

## USING ADVERBS

It doesn't seem very long ago since giving birth to Valerie. It's barely been a year. In hospital, I remember thinking that I'd definitely need drugs. But I wasn't really thinking straight and lost the opportunity. While giving birth, I was painfully aware of every spasm in my body. I can hardly believe that what was once so tiny became so big, and pushed through me so violently.

## USING CLICHÉS

Time has flown by since giving birth to Valerie. I remember thinking that I'd gotten myself in way over my head. I'd put off asking for an epidural to the best of my ability, but then when I decided I needed it, it was too late. I can't believe Valerie was once as small as a speck of dust, and grew so big, and then pushed through such a small opening. The pain, let me tell you, was off the charts.

## UNIQUE EXAMPLE

I gave birth to Valerie a year ago. That year has gone by so fast I often wonder if I still have toes. I can still feel my legs in those stirrups—the sweaty doctor sucking the entire universe through my spasming black hole, too late to ask for chemical courage. Muscles pulled from my spine, my thighs to my pelvis, every push a deliberate infliction of pain. What began as an insignificant seed, thrust itself through me like a fist tearing through fabric.

# EXAMPLE 23

**Adverb:** deadly

**Cliché:** never felt so (adj) in one's life

## USING ADVERB

I'm deadly relaxed.

## USING CLICHÉ

I have never felt so relaxed in my life. I feel like I'm going to lose consciousness!

## UNIQUE EXAMPLE

My body sinks into the sofa like a hollow log in quicksand.

# EXAMPLE 24

**Adverbs:** defiantly • slightly

**Clichés:** find the key to one's heart • the lights are on but nobody's home • windows of one's soul

## USING ADVERBS

I lean forward slightly, looking defiantly into his eyes. But they seem full of so much nothingness. I guess he just doesn't want to let me in.

## USING CLICHÉS

I lean forward, close enough to peer into the windows of his soul. The lights are on, but there doesn't seem to be anyone home. I guess I'll never find the key to his heart.

## UNIQUE EXAMPLE

I lean forward. But I can't see past my fishbowl reflection in his eyes' watery sheen. They're like double-glazed windows. You can see through them, but you can't hear what's happening on the other side.

# EXAMPLE 25

**Adverb:** simultaneously

**Cliché:** all at once

## USING ADVERB

All five people speak simultaneously.

## USING CLICHÉ

The five people speak all at once.

## UNIQUE EXAMPLE

Their five voices overlap like a tuning orchestra.

# EXAMPLE 26

**Adverb:** offensively

**Cliché:** dust bunnies

## USING ADVERB

My bed sheets are offensively dusty.

## USING CLICHÉ

My bed sheets are full of dust bunnies.

## UNIQUE EXAMPLE

Getting into bed is like stepping into a vacuum cleaner bag.

# EXAMPLE 27

**Adverbs:** basically • eternally • highly • mainly • mightily

**Clichés:** call the shots • different shapes and sizes • do as one pleases • leave one's mark on (n)

## USING ADVERBS

He mainly wants to become influential, and to be eternally free to follow as many different paths as he desires, to basically see, and do, the undiscovered, to become highly respected and call out mightily to the world: "I am your president!"

## USING CLICHÉS

He wants to leave his mark on the world; to forever be free to do as he pleases, to follow paths of all different shapes and sizes; to make the world's population gloat over him, and know that he is the only one who calls the shots.

## UNIQUE EXAMPLE

He wants to make some noise; enough to bulldoze a permanent exit from this dead-end life, giving access to a new and undiscovered highway; to hear the influence of his motivation, his determination, echo through a football stadium like a thousand bass drums beating the thunderous rhythm of world domination.

# EXAMPLE 28

**Adverb:** unusually

**Cliché:** hard as rock

## USING ADVERB

Donna's hairdo looks unusually stiff.

## USING CLICHÉ

Donna's hairdo looks as hard as rock.

## UNIQUE EXAMPLE

Donna's hairdo looks as if it's been sprayed in position since 1982.

# EXAMPLE 29

**Adverb:** madly

**Cliché:** like bees to honey

## USING ADVERB

Women are madly attracted to Frank.

## USING CLICHÉ

Frank attracts women like bees to honey.

## UNIQUE EXAMPLE

What an atheist is to a Jehovah's Witness, Frank is to women.

# EXAMPLE 30

**Adverbs:** antagonistically • boldly

**Clichés:** crumble under pressure • smile like a Cheshire Cat • stare someone down

## USING ADVERBS

Adam smiles, and antagonistically stares at me. But I boldly refuse to succumb to his manipulation.

## USING CLICHÉS

Adam smiles like a Cheshire Cat and tries to stare me down. But I will not crumble under the pressure.

## UNIQUE EXAMPLE

With an arrogant grin, Adam glares at me. He may be fire. But I am not ice.

# EXAMPLE 31

**Adverbs:** eagerly • erratically • proudly

**Clichés:** have ants in one's pants • pride and joy
• scan every inch

## USING ADVERBS

Her eyes move erratically, left to right, eagerly searching for the perfect position on the wall to proudly hang her new piece of art.

## USING CLICHÉS

She scans every inch of our four walls like she's got ants in her pants, trying to locate a spot to hang her art. It's her new pride and joy.

## UNIQUE EXAMPLE

Her eyes dart from wall to wall, as if hunting down a mosquito, trying to determine the perfect position to display her very first "masterpiece."

# EXAMPLE 32

**Adverb:** tenderly

**Cliché:** tingling up and down one's spine

## USING ADVERB

He tenderly stroked my cheek and it made my skin feel all tingly.

## USING CLICHÉ

When he stroked my cheek, I felt tingling up and down my spine.

## UNIQUE EXAMPLE

When he stroked my cheek, it tingled as if he was transferring energy into my soul.

# EXAMPLE 33

**Adverb:** swiftly

**Cliché:** in one fell swoop

## USING ADVERB

Eva swiftly grabs her thesis from the drawer.

## USING CLICHÉ

In one fell swoop, Eva snatches her thesis from the drawer.

## UNIQUE EXAMPLE

Eva scoops her thesis from the drawer like an eagle catching prey.

# EXAMPLE 34

**Adverbs:** consciously • consistently • fondly
• idly • merely • never • reluctantly • soon

**Clichés:** collect dust • come to terms with • have a mind of
one's own • only a matter of time • stay in shape • toy with an
idea • withstand the test of time

## USING ADVERBS

I used to think fondly of my second-hand acoustic guitar
and how she consistently stayed in tune. I pretended she was
consciously aware of her existence, and determined to never
give up. When I reluctantly sold her, I felt better knowing she
wouldn't sit idly in a shop window. She would soon convince
another person to play her again by merely tempting them
with her beauty.

## USING CLICHÉS

I used to love my second-hand acoustic guitar for how she
withstood the test of time. I liked to toy with the idea that
she had a mind of her own, and that's how she stayed in such
good shape. When I sold her, it helped me come to terms
with letting her go, knowing she wouldn't sit in a corner
collecting dust; knowing it would only be a matter of time
before her unique splendour tempted somebody to play her
again.

## UNIQUE EXAMPLE

I used to admire my second-hand acoustic guitar as if she were a rare antique chair, contemplating her own remarkable existence, reminiscing about all the generations of people who had used her before me. When I sold her, it was comforting to think that no matter how many times people walked past her in the display window, she understood that everyone appreciated her beauty, her universal function. That one day, someone would purchase her, cherish her, and play her with love.

# NOW IT'S YOUR TURN

## CHANGE THE FOLLOWING INTO SOMETHING UNIQUE WITHOUT THE USE OF ADVERBS OR CLICHÉS:

1. I wake up. My lips slowly become unstuck as I yawn. I have a feeling that something is terribly wrong. I quickly sit upright in bed and gaze out the window. It's raining cats and dogs.

2. Lila swiftly packed up her belongings and fled the hotel in the blink of an eye. There was no way she was going to let herself get caught now. Not after travelling through hell and high water to finally find these diamonds.

3. I was so surprised at his announcement that my jaw dropped! My friend must have been so embarrassed by my behaviour because she had to physically close my mouth for me. How dare he do this? Who does he think he is to drop such a bombshell?

# INDEX OF ADVERBS

# INDEX OF CLICHÉS

# ACKNOWLEDGEMENTS

This is the part where I'm supposed to thank everyone that helped me with this book. So here goes ...

Thank you to everyone who helped me with this book.

Okay, seriously now ...

Many thanks go to the authors who were my guinea pigs and offered invaluable feedback on early drafts of this book. Names off the top of my head are: Leigh Talbert Moore, Matthew MacNish, Glynis Smy, Dawn Ius, Becca Puglisi, Debbie Young, Talli Roland, and Angela Macintosh. If I've forgotten you, I apologize for my lack of record-keeping in this department!

Of course, I mustn't forget Amie McCracken, an inspiring young woman and powerhouse, who not only helped revise this 2nd Edition, but who's also been my go-to editor, typesetter, and eBook formatter, since we met in 2011. My life would be in a shambles without her. Thank you for being such a great colleague and friend, Amie.

*If you found this book helpful, it would be extremely appreciated if you could post a review at the retailer you purchased it from.*

### *Interested in my upcoming titles?*
*You can sign up for my newsletter at*
***jessicabellauthor.com*** *to stay up-to-date.*

# Independent Publishing Assistance

All your book production needs at your fingertips.

www.indiepublishingassist.com

www.ingramcontent.com/pod-product-compliance
Lightning Source LLC
Chambersburg PA
CBHW021219020426
42331CB00003B/385